DECODING GOD'S
DIVINE
CALENDAR

Decoding God's Divine Calendar

Chris James

WATCHMEN BROADCASTING

www.WatchmenChristianTV.com

Decoding God's Divine Calendar
by Chris James

Printed in the United States of America

ISBN 978-1532961977

Cover Design & Interior Layout: AJ Design and Marketing, LLC

Dedication

This book is dedicated to the partners and volunteers of Watchmen Broadcasting, past, present, and future and to those who have supported this ministry financially and with prayers. To those who spoke a word of encouragement when the enemy would come and attack me, my family, and the ministry as a whole, your words of encouragement, your prayers, and the gifts you gave at just the right time made this book a reality. Thank you. I dedicate this book to my parents who taught me the value of God's Holy Word. Thank you for challenging me as a child to read the Bible and teach you what I learned. This book is also dedicated to Dorothy Spaulding who saw a rough young man and took a chance on him. Her leadership and encouragement helped mold me into the person I am today.

I also dedicate this book to my wife, Tamara, who made me write it. She pushed and pushed and saw something in me I never knew was there. Thank you for making me expand my tent and move into the call God has placed on my life. Tamara, I love you and appreciate your tenacity for the things of God.

Introduction

In January of 2013, a local pastor named Ray Popham, a good friend and a true man of God, came to Watchmen Broadcasting a television station serving the Augusta, Georgia market with a word that it is the *Year of the Camel*. He began to explain that the year was actually 5773 according to the Hebraic Calendar. Little did I know, his teaching would forever alter my life. He would instill a way of thinking that would change the way I study and see the word of God. After his teaching, I began to seek out the meaning of the following years myself. I would go into study and look at the meaning of each letter and of each number to find deeper meanings. The word of God began to become clear and mysteries unveiled.

While studying the meanings of each number, I began to realize that God has made it plain for anyone to predict what He is doing and the timing of His Divine Calendar. The word of God tells us in 2 Timothy 2:15:

> *"Study to shew thyself approved unto God, a workman that needeth not to be ashamed, rightly dividing the word of truth."*

This scripture states we are to dive into the word of God and dissect it to find the deeper meanings of the words. The only way I knew to study prior to Pastor Popham's teaching was strictly with a concordance. Concordances are great study tools, but they are just the base level of digging deep into the meaning of God's word. If we truly want to understand the word of God, we have to realize it was written for and by God's chosen people. Accepting this knowledge, we now have to look at the customs and ideology of the people who were divinely inspired to write the Bible.

In the Hebrew alphabet, there are 22 letters and each letter has a numeric value. The Hebrew word for *letter* is *ot* (אות), which can also mean *sign* or *wonder*. If each letter in Hebrew holds its own sign and wonder, then when we combine letters together and take each meaning we get a much better understanding of what God is really doing. We have the ability to decipher the times and seasons. God has placed everything He has done and will do in His word, and He has given us the ability to see what is coming long before it happens. His people have always had the ability to do so. The Jewish people have done it for centuries, and now you and I can do it as well.

Some of these concepts are difficult for those of us unfamiliar with the Jewish culture and the Hebrew language. I recommend you review the content at <u>hebrew4christians.com</u> and <u>chabad.org</u> to give you an entry into understanding the beautiful Jewish culture.

In this book, I will take you on a journey to see what God is doing according to His Divine Calendar. We will specifically focus on 2013 – 2017, or 5773 – 5777. Get out your highlighter and a notepad, and let's see what God has been doing.

TABLE OF CONTENTS

Chapter I

THE CAMELS ARE COMING

In January of 2013, Pastor Ray Popham came to the Watchmen Broadcasting studios to be on our flagship program Club 36 with a word for 2013. He told Dorothy, the host and CEO of Watchmen Broadcasting, that it is the Year of the Camel. You may be asking yourself, "What is he talking about?" Has he been studying the Chinese New Years? The answer is no. According to the Chinese Zodiac, 2013 was the year of the Snake. Also, they do not use a camel anywhere in their Zodiac. Pastor Popham began to reveal that the year was 5773 according to the Hebraic Calendar. The Jews believe that the earth was created 5773 years ago according to the time of Pastor Popham's teaching. As Pastor Popham continued to teach, Dorothy got so excited that she made her entire staff change the theme of the Praise-A-Thon, which was scheduled the following week, to "The Camels Are Coming". Many of the staff thought she was crazy to call the Praise-A-Thon "The Camels Are Coming". However, she is the boss and everyone sucked it up and began to make the necessary changes. As the staff came together to honor what God placed in her heart, God began to move in a way no one had ever seen before in the ministry. Before I share the move of God that happened at Watchmen Broadcasting, I want you to understand the meaning of the Year of the Camel.

To understand the Year of the Camel, you first have to realize our way of telling time has been altered, and the current calendar we use, the Gregorian Calendar, is just one of many ways our adversary has tried to manipulate time to prevent us from understanding the timing of God. According to the Hebraic Calendar, the New Year begins in the seventh month of Tishri. In the year 5773, that just so happened to be September 17, 2012. By the time we were learning about God's New Year, we were already 3½ months into it.

The Year 5773 took place between September 17, 2012 and September 2, 2013. The Jews look at the last two numbers to find the meaning of each year. In the case of 5773, they look at the 7 and the 3. To be more specific, they look at 70 and 3. The Hebrew letter for 70 is *Ayin*, the 16th letter of the Hebrew alphabet.  The letter *Ayin* literally means *eye* or *to see* and by extension, *to understand and obey*. The Jews also believe that any number multiplied by ten is the fulfillment of that number or that number perfected. The picture of the *Ayin* is that of two eyes connected to one optic nerve.

The number 70 shows up a lot in scripture:

- 70 souls went to Egypt,
- 70 elders of Israel saw the God of Israel on Mt. Sinai,
- 70 sacrifices made for the nations (during the feast of Sukkot)
- Israel was exiled 70 years in Babylon.
- In Jewish tradition, there are 70 members of the Sanhedrin,
- 70 words of Kaddish,
- 70 "faces of Torah,"
- 70 Names of God,
- 70 birth pangs until the coming of Mashiach[1]

---

1   Parsons, John J. "The Letter Ayin." The Letter Ayin. Hebrew for Christians. Web. 25 Apr. 2016.

The Eye(s) of the Lord

In the Scriptures, God's intimate knowledge of our lives is sometimes referred to as the "Eye of the Lord." Adonai's eyes are in every place, observing both the good and the evil (Prov. 15:3). The Lord's eyes focus throughout the whole earth to defend the righteous (2 Chr. 16:9) and to sustain and deliver those who are hoping in His faithful mercy. We will go into more depth about *Ayin* and its significance in later chapters.

Now that we have a basic understanding of the *Ayin* (70) and what it means, we will look at the number 3 in Hebrew. The  number 3 in Hebrew is the Gimel. Gimel means camel, bridge, weaning, benevolence. Gimel is the 3rd letter in the Jewish Alphabet and represents the number 3. It is pictured as a camel and as a rich man chasing down a poor man to give charity.

Camels show up in the Bible as a way to transport people and things; they are a sign of provision. These animals are strong and can carry a great weight. They can go long periods of time and great distances without water. They can survive in harsh conditions and were the animal of choice in Bible times for traveling great distances. In Genesis 24, we read a story about Abraham sending his servant to find his son, Isaac, a wife. Verse 10 states:

> *And the servant took ten camels of the camels of his master, and departed; for all the goods of his master were in his hand: and he arose, and went to Mesopotamia, unto the city of Nahor.*
>
> Genesis 24:10

I love this verse of scripture. We see that Abraham had a servant, a man he trusted more than anyone. He trusted this servant so much he gave him access to everything he had and sent him on his way to find his son, Isaac, a wife. Is there someone in your life you trust so much that you would entrust them to find a wife for your son? I have people in my life that I love dearly and trust them with my life, but I don't think there is anyone I would trust to find my only son a wife. The man Abraham chose knew Abraham, and he knew Abraham's God. He traveled to Mesopotamia and parked the ten camels at a well where all the available women would come to gather water for their families.

While he was there, he made a petition to Abraham's God to let a woman offer to water his master's camels as a sign that she is the woman God ordained to be Isaac's wife. Rebekah comes along; the servant asks for water, and she gives him water and offers to water his camels. God answered his prayer. We pick up with verse 22:

> *And it came to pass, as the camels had done drinking, that the man took a golden earring of half a shekel weight, and two bracelets for her hands of ten shekels weight of gold;*
>
> Genesis 24:22

The servant bestows gifts upon Rebekah after his prayer was answered. We begin to see what Abraham's servant had taken from Abraham's treasury. The first thing he gave to Rebekah was a gold earring and 2 gold bracelets. Rebekah takes Abraham's servant home to meet her parents. The servant explained his purpose for being in Mesopotamia and tells the events involving Rebekah and the camels. Rebekah's family gave her to the servant to take back to Isaac to be his wife. In verse 53, we see what else Abraham's servant brought on the journey:

*And the servant brought forth jewels of silver, and jewels of
gold, and raiment, and gave them to Rebekah: he gave also to
her brother and to her mother precious things.*

Genesis 24:53

The servant brought things of great value on his master's
camels. In the New Testament of the Bible, we learn of the birth
of Jesus and of the wise men who came to see Him.

*And when they were come into the house, they saw the young
child with Mary his mother, and fell down, and worshipped
him: and when they had opened their treasures, they
presented unto him gifts; gold, and frankincense, and myrrh.*

Mathew 2:11

These men who studied the stars were called Magi, which is
where we get the word magician from today. They were extremely
wise men, and it is believed, based on the gifts they gave to Jesus,
that they were from Arabia which is referred to in the Bible as
the East. These men would have traveled in a large number as to
detour being robbed. They also set out on a journey not knowing
where they were going, or how long it would take to get there.
They would have carried provisions to set up camp, pay for food,
lodging, or any other needs they may run into. This is believed

to be a caravan of at least 14 men. A few verses later we learn that God tells Joseph it is time for him to pack up the family and move to Egypt. God provided everything needed for the move.

THE YEAR OF THE CAMEL OR THE CAMELS ARE COMING

We now take the meaning of the *Ayin* (70) and the Gimel (3), and we apply that to the stories mentioned above to get the meaning of 5773. The Camels are coming bringing great provision to those who have been faithful unto the Lord. He is watching and He will continue to watch you. He is going to bless those who have not lost faith that He will do what He said He would do. He is sending a great wave of Camels carrying provision over a 3 year period that will sustain you and set you up for a great inheritance. He is the rich man chasing you down to give you charity. God has set a season aside to bless those who have been faithful to Him and who will not be moved no matter what comes their way.

The same month Pastor Ray Popham shared this word with us the largest gift this ministry has ever seen came in. An anonymous giver gave $604,437.04 to the ministry for our building. We were completely blown away. I remember my wife Tamara opening the envelope and letting out a loud scream. I ran to see what the commotion was all about, and she could not even speak. Her lips were stammering trying to form words, but they would not come out. She handed me the letter and the check that was addressed to Watchmen Broadcasting. I was speechless. Finally, Tamara was able to compose herself to call Dorothy to let her know about the gift. The first camel had come and it was a big camel. God had dropped in Dorothy's spirit the importance of the on time word, "The Camels Are Coming."

For the next 3 months, Dorothy would try to negotiate a deal with the owner of the building we are currently in. God had hardened his heart. Frustrated over the situation Dorothy, her husband Russell, Tamara, and I began to pray about the situation, and I felt the Lord drop in my spirit we should pursue the abandoned Food Lion building next door. Since I have been in this ministry, I remember Dorothy and Russell talking about owning both properties. The owner of the Food Lion was asking

1.2 million for the Food Lion and the Sub Terminal building at the edge of the property. I felt we were to offer $400,000 for the property and see what God would do. Dorothy and Tamara were in agreement. Dorothy made the necessary calls and one miracle after another happened. The owner of the Food Lion owed $650,000 on the property. He stated he has always wanted the ministry to have the building but was not in a position to give it to us for free. He stated that if the bank would allow him to separate the Sub Terminal from the Food Lion we would have a deal. God moved, the bank transferred $250,000 worth of debt to the Sub Terminal. The Sub Terminal is not worth anywhere close to $250,000. We had a partner step up and pay the closing cost of $1,000 for the survey and paperwork to be filed. We had Dumpster Depot give us ten dumpsters free of charge a value of $5,000. We had over 50 volunteers show up and strip the building down to the base structure. We also replaced the roof. All of this took place within a six-month period.

I want you to think back to September 17, 2012 – September 4, 2013 and remind yourself what provisions God brought into your life. What did God do during this time that set you up for success? You were in God's perfect timing and you didn't even know it. God has a calendar, and He has you all over it.

Chapter 2

SETUP FOR FUTURE YEARS

Earlier, I mentioned a three-year period of blessings. I want to expound on that for you. I want you to think of each decade as a cake and each year as an ingredient that is needed to make the cake. When making a cake, you do not disregard the eggs, flour, sugar, milk or any other ingredient. Without each ingredient, the cake would not be fit to eat. Using this analogy we cannot disregard the value of 5773 when going into 5774. Without 5773, there would be no 5774. As we move forward, we will continue to accredit 5773 and add each year as a new ingredient for the overall decade.

After the experiences the ministry encountered in 2013, I wanted to get a head start and learn the meaning of the following year. I also began to look into the Jewish Feast Rosh Hashanah since it is the Jewish New Year. As I began to research this Jewish Feast, I learned that each year on Rosh Hashanah "all inhabitants of the world pass

before God like a flock of sheep," and it is decreed in the heavenly

court "*who shall **live**, and who shall die … who shall be impoverished,*

*and who shall be **enriched**; who shall fall and who shall **rise**.*" This is

also the day we proclaim God **King of the Universe**.

> ²⁴*Speak unto the children of Israel, saying, In the seventh*
> *month, in the first day of the month, shall ye have a sabbath,*
> *a memorial of blowing of trumpets, an holy convocation.* ²⁵*Ye*
> *shall do no servile work therein: but ye shall offer an offering*
> *made by fire unto the Lord.* ²⁶*And the Lord spake unto Moses,*
> *saying,* ²⁷*Also on the tenth day of this seventh month there*
> *shall be a day of atonement: it shall be an holy convocation*
> *unto you; and ye shall afflict your souls, and offer an offering*
> *made by fire unto the Lord.* ²⁸*And ye shall do no work in that*
> *same day: for it is a day of atonement, to make an atonement*
> *for you before the Lord your God.*
>
> Leviticus 23:24–28

The Jews believe on Rosh Hashanah God opens the book of

life and judges your past year and what will lie in store for you in

the coming year. This is a time when the Jews reflect on the past

year. They fast, pray, and repent. Rosh Hashanah starts a ten-day

period where we must make things right with God before we go into the new year. During this 10 day period, we must pray and repent for all of our actions over the past year. While researching this Jewish festival, I found out that in order to apologize to God we must pray, repent, and give to charity. True repentance is regretting your sin, resolving not to commit the sin again in the future, and confessing your sin to God.

The tenth day of this period is Yom Kippur, the Day of Awe. This is when God closes the Book of Life and seals what He has written until the next year. I truly believe that for those who grab hold of this revelation there will be true deliverance. If you have been dealing with something over and over again, now is the time to be set free. God has appointed times and seasons to deal with things and now is the time.

Understanding the times and seasons of God is vital to truly fulfill the call He has placed on your life. If you wanted to be a contestant on American Idol, you would want to know when the tryouts are. It wouldn't do you any good to show up two or three months after the tryouts. You would have missed your opportunity. In essence, by not knowing the timing of God, we can miss our day of visitation.

I say all this about Rosh Hashanah and Yom Kippur only to encourage you to look at things from a Jewish perspective. When God speaks to us through His word, He does it through pictures. Every letter in the Hebrew alphabet has its own meaning and is tied to a picture. Understanding that God has ordained from the foundation of the world that we are to come before Him at specific times is key to understanding everything you read as we move forward.

Chapter 3

5774, The Year of the Open Door

5774 began September 5, 2013 and ended September 24, 2014. As before, we will look at the last two numbers of the year 7 and 4 or 70 and 4. 70 is *Ayin* and 4 is *Dalet*. To refresh, the letter *Ayin* literally means *eye* or *to see* and by extension, *to understand and obey*. The letter *Dalet* is the fourth letter in the Hebrew alphabet. *Dalet* literally means *door, opening, entry,* or *pathway.* The *Dalet* is pictured as the opening to a tent. The year 5774 means The Year of the Open Door. What does this year mean? Why is a door opening this year, and what is behind this door that God is opening this year? That is a great question; we will look at Psalm 24 for the answer.

> [1]*A Psalm of David. The earth is the* LORD*'s, and the fullness thereof; the world, and they that dwell therein.*
>
> [2]*For he hath founded it upon the seas, and established it upon the floods.*

³*Who shall ascend into the hill of the* LORD*? or who shall stand in his holy place?*

⁴*He that hath clean hands, and a pure heart; who hath not lifted up his soul unto vanity, nor sworn deceitfully.*

⁵*He shall receive the blessing from the* LORD*, and righteousness from the God of his salvation.*

⁶*This is the generation of them that seek him, that seek thy face, O Jacob.*

Selah.

⁷***Lift up your heads, O ye gates; and be ye lift up, ye everlasting doors; and the King of glory shall come in.***

⁸*Who is this King of glory? The* LORD *strong and mighty, the* LORD *mighty in battle.*

⁹***Lift up your heads, O ye gates; even lift them up, ye everlasting doors; and the King of glory shall come in.***

¹⁰*Who is this King of glory? The* LORD *of hosts, he is the King of glory.*

Selah.

Psalm 24 **(emphasis mine)**

I want to draw your attention to verse 7, "Lift up your heads, O ye gates; and be ye lift up, ye everlasting doors; and the King of glory shall come in." The verse is repeated word for word in verse 9. The fact that the verse is repeated means it is significant.

Here God has called you a gate. Lift up your head, O ye gate. You are a form of a doorway, an entrance. God tells us here to lift our heads up. Anytime we are told to look up or go up it relates to making our focus God. The scripture then calls us everlasting doors. Two times in this verse we are called two different entryways. What is the purpose of us being an entryway? So the King of glory shall come in. God created us for one reason; He wanted a relationship. He wants to spend time with us in the cool of the day. He wants to hear about our day. He cares about the things that we do that no one else does.

> *7 Then said Jesus unto them again, "Verily, verily, I say unto you, I am the door of the sheep. 8 All that ever came before me are thieves and robbers: but the sheep did not hear them. 9 I am the door: by me if any man enter in, he shall be saved, and shall go in and out, and find pasture."*
>
> John 10:7–9

Jesus came to restore our relationship with the Father. He called Himself a door and the only way to the Father is through Him and through Him alone.

I know thy works: behold, I have set before thee an open door,
and no man can shut it: for thou hast a little strength, and
hast kept my word, and hast not denied my name.

Revelation 3:8

Using these verses, let's now declare the meaning of the Year of the Open Door. 5774, *Ayin Dalet*, The Year of the Open Door is a year of the double portion. This year new relationships were established and old relationships were restored. Many ran away from the restoration process in fear, not realizing what God wanted to do was promote them through these relationships. God uses people to promote one another, and 5774 was a pivotal year. God brought provision in 5773, and in 5774 He created the opportunity for promotion. The relationships that were most damaged God used to promote those who were able to let the past go. Those who let go of hurts and bitterness from the past, are those God can trust and promote. He gave them a double portion.

You are a doorway. You allow things in and out. You decide who will be promoted and who will not. By the choices you make and the company you keep, through relationships, you decide what you allow in your home, your work place, in your car, and in your spirit. You decide who you promote into your life. God wants to open up the door of relationships to you so He can use these relationships to promote you to the calling He has given you. Some relationships hurt. God does not intend these relationships for us to be abused or taken advantage of, but rather that we would be humbled through them.

> *The king's heart is in the hand of the Lord, as the rivers of water: he turneth it whithersoever he will.*
>
> Proverbs 21:1

Your employer, your pastor, your family, and the government are in the hand of the Lord. He will use whosoever He wants to promote those who have not lost the faith, those who have not given up on the dreams and words given to them by God Himself. Your promotion is so important to Him that He has made someone take notice of you even when they didn't think you were worth taking notice of.

In January of 2014, the National Religious Broadcasters (NRB), an organization that advances biblical truth, promotes excellence in media, and defends free speech, called Dorothy and asked if she would mind if they nominated her for the TV Advisory Committee. Dorothy didn't tell me the NRB called. I heard part of the story, and I was hurt and even offended by the situation. The previous year Dorothy asked the chairman to open a door for me to get involved with the TV Committee. They actually placed my name as a write in on the ballot the year before. When the votes were counted, I did not have enough votes to be on the committee. I had wished no one would have said anything to me about it. I prayed and told the Lord that He knows what is best for the NRB and best for me and what was best for Dorothy. I let it go. It was hard at the time because I wanted to pick it up, but I told God it was His, not mine to deal with. The time finally came to vote, and I really wanted to avoid going to the meeting because I did not want to rain on Dorothy's parade as she would have been voted onto the TV Committee. Dorothy made me go to the meeting. When she was announced as being on the ballot, she stood up and said, "It has always been a desire of my heart to serve on this committee, but I would like to substitute my name for Chris James. He is my son-in-law and he would serve this committee well as he has been an answer to prayer to my ministry." Do you know how they say hindsight is 20/20? I realized she agreed to put her name on the ballot just to have the opportunity to promote me publicly and give me her endorsement. Only a few people who were voting knew me. I never would have been voted onto the committee had she not put her name on the ballot and given up something she desperately wanted. I was promoted because of a relationship.

Just a side note: Two years later, this year in fact, Dorothy has been nominated to be on the board of NRB, not on a committee, but on the board. God not only used Dorothy to promote me, but because she promoted me, she herself was promoted to an even higher level than she thought would have even been possible. God is in the business of promoting His people when they are faithful and trust Him with their whole hearts.

I told you earlier that each year ties into the next. I also told you there would be a three year period of camels that would come, bringing provision for those who were faithful to the Lord. Two more camels came during this Hebrew year of 5774. The ministry had more money come in this year than ever before.

Unfortunately, it was all designated to a building and could not be used anywhere else. Running a TV ministry is very expensive. To run the TV station appropriately, we need $3,000 to come in the mail each day. That's $1,095,000 a year to run a 24 hour a day ministry. We fell behind on all of the monthly bills. There were months where the only thing the ministry paid was the staff.

We had fallen behind on our building rent. We were $16,000 behind. We had fallen behind in the past, but never this far. The building owner called and gave an ultimatum. Dorothy took the call; she began to tell him that we would have it because God would supply if he would just be patient with us. The owner stated that maybe God is no longer behind what we are doing in the ministry. Needless to say, we knew only God could move this mountain. A few days later, the 14th of November, Tamara woke up in a panic attack over the finances. These attacks had been happening for the past several months to the point there were days that Tamara didn't sleep at all. Tamara would average only three hours of sleep at night if she was lucky. This night was different; when Tamara woke up in a panic attack something rose up in her, and she just simply prayed: "Father, I know you are in control and I set this care on you. You will supply what we need." She then went back to sleep and slept all the way through the night. The next morning we dropped the kids off at school and headed to the post office box to collect the mail. When we got there, there were only three envelopes in the mail box. Instead of getting discouraged, Tamara looked at me and said, "It only takes one to make a difference." She opened the first envelope; it was for $30.00. She opened the second one; it was $20.00. She looked at the last one and said again, "It only takes one.' She opened it and sighed a huge sigh of relief. Our first camel of 5774 showed up. Inside the envelope was a check for $25,000. We paid the back rent off in full.

Seven days later the ministry received another large anonymous gift of $378,428.61. This gift came at a time when the ministry needed it most. This gift was not assigned to any project. It was available to use wherever it was needed most. Remember this ministry needs to bring in $3,000 a day to operate. Over the past year, the ministry had accrued a debt of $100,000. We pinched every penny possible. We were down to one working wireless microphone. Imagine trying to do a job with missing or broken tools. It is next to impossible. This gift came the week of Thanksgiving, and we were giving thanks. Tamara is the bookkeeper at Watchmen Broadcasting, and she had really begun to feel the burden of the finances. I was giving thanks that my wife would be able to sleep without the enemy attacking her in this area anymore. Tamara paid off every bill, and the harassing phone calls stopped. We serve a good God. He doesn't always show up the way we want Him to; however, He is true to His word, He never leaves us nor forsakes us.

Think back over the year 5774, September 5, 2013 – September 24, 2014. Did God promote you in some way? If so, write down how.

_____

_____

_____

_____

_____

If your provision in 5773 didn't come, how would that have prevented the promotion of 5774? Who did God use to promote you? As I am writing this now, I never put the dates together before as to my promotion to the NRB TV Committee. What have you overlooked that God has done for you? Take a few minutes and just thank Him for His mercy and grace.

Chapter 4

5775, The Year of the Open Window

5775 began September 25, 2014 and ended September 13, 2015. We will look at the last two numbers the 7 and 5 or the 70 and 5. *Ayin* (70) *Hey* (5). Remember *Ayin* literally means *eye* or *to see* and by extension, *to understand and obey*. *Hey* is the fifth letter in the Hebrew alphabet and also represents the number 5. *Hey* means *window, look, revel, breath,* and *behold*. The number *Hey* is pictured as a *Dalet* (4) with a hand reaching out. It can mean returning to God by means of the transforming power of the Spirit. This in essence is a picture of the Spirit of God dwelling in us. As we allow God to come into our tent or our heart in a greater way, He will move upon us; **we will arise, produce, and prevail!** Before God can move in our society, our government, and our churches, He must first move upon the hearts of His people. The hand of

God must revive us. He must move upon the tent of our heart, reanimating us. After this mighty in dwelling, we shall advance into our proper authority and calling. Many are calling for revival, but they believe for an influx of new Christians. The meaning of revival is to take something dead and to reanimate it or bring it back to life. How can we expect new Christians until we are brought back to life and fall back in love with our Holy Father?

When God moves, you must expect Him to move in you first. You will be empowered if you have been faithful. **He will ARISE in you and you will turn situations around. You will decree and declare the God in Me is power to prevail!** God is calling you out of the four walls of the church. He will give you power to prevail at work, in civic realms, and within your social circles. **You will arise in your expertise! Arise in your mastery! Arise in your influence! Arise in His Glory!** For some this was a year of double portion and for those who have been faithful, a year of quadruple portion.

The word *window* shows up in 42 verses in the King James Version of the Bible. The majority of the times it shows up it is referenced as a literal window as in this passage from Chronicles:

> *And it came to pass, as the ark of the covenant of the Lord*
> *came to the city of David, that Michal the daughter of Saul*
> *looking out a window saw king David dancing and playing:*
> *and she despised him in her heart.*
>
> 1 Chronicles 15:29

The other references to windows occur when they are described in their design:

> *And there were narrow windows to the little chambers, and*
> *their posts within the gate round about, and likewise to the*
> *arches: and windows were round about inward: and upon*
> *each post were palm trees.*
>
> Ezekiel 40:16

Let's stop here for just a minute and reflect on what is the purpose of a window in the natural. Windows let in light; they allow fresh air to come in. They can be opened or closed. When closed they prevent undesired things from getting in. Now, let's look at what a window does and apply that to the supernatural. Windows bring in a spiritual refreshing or awakening. They bring a light or an enlightening to a situation that was previously hidden. Just by this description, we can see how powerful a window can be when God gets involved in our lives, but this is just bare minimum of the true power of a window.

The most well known reference to windows in the Bible would probably be God opening the windows of Heaven. One of the meanings is when God opens the Heavens and rain falls on the earth. We see this in the story of Noah in Genesis chapters 7 and 8. Another time we see God opening the Heavens is in 2 Kings 7. The nation of Israel is in a great famine as the Syrian army is camped around the city. God tells Elisha to go to the king and tell him tomorrow at this time a measure of fine flour will be sold for a shekel and two measures of barley for a shekel in the gate of Samaria. A trusted advisor to the king states to Elisha that even if God opened the windows of Heaven how could this happen. Elisha tells the king's advisor that he will see it happen, but never be able to partake of the Lord's blessing. Meanwhile, four lepers were starving outside of the gates of the city. They reasoned if they stayed outside of the gate they would die due to the famine. They decided to go to the Syrians hoping for pity and a chance of a meal. As the lepers moved toward the Syrian army, God showed up and caused the shuffling feet of the lepers to sound like a great army was upon them. The Syrians became terrified, fleeing for their lives and leaving everything behind. The lepers ate and drank their fill taking for themselves; then they go to the king and tell him what had happened. The king's advisor was placed at the gate to distribute the goods and was trampled to death just as Elisha had said. God opened the windows of Heaven and saved His chosen people with four lepers. Probably, the most well known verse about the windows of Heaven is in Malachi 3:10:

> *Bring ye all the tithes into the storehouse, that there may be meat in mine house, and prove me now herewith, saith the Lord of hosts, if I will not open you the windows of heaven, and pour you out a blessing, that there shall not be room enough to receive it.*
>
> Malachi 3:10

We see here God wants to bless His people, but He requires us to be obedient and have faith in Him. God wants us to trust Him, and He also wants us to prove our trustworthiness to Him by following His commands.

After reading all of the scriptures related to windows in the Bible, I found a very interesting use for windows. In the second chapter of Joshua, we see Joshua has sent two spies into Jericho. They find Rahab, and she hides them. She then asked them to deal kindly with her when they overtake the city. They agreed and we see in verse 15:

> *Then she let them down by a cord through the window: for her house was upon the town wall, and she dwelt upon the wall.*
>
> Joshua 2:15

God used Rahab to deliver the two spies through her window. Here we see a window is a way of escape. Deliverance can come through a window. Not only did God deliver the two spies, but God used the very same window in Joshua 2:18 to deliver Rahab and her entire family.

> *Behold, when we come into the land, thou shall bind this line of scarlet thread in the window which thou didst let us down by: and thou shalt bring thy father, and thy mother, and thy brethren, and all thy father's household, home unto thee.*
>
> Joshua 2:18

The very method Rahab used to deliver the two spies, the spies used to deliver her entire family.

While researching windows in scripture, I also found where David was delivered and set free from Saul by a window.

> *So Michal let David down through a window: and he went, and fled, and escaped.*
>
> 1 Samuel 19:12

The future king of all Israel was in need of an escape, and God provided it through Saul's daughter, the very bloodline of the one that was trying to kill him. Remember, I explained earlier that each year works with the next. In 5774, the focus was on relationships, and in 5775, the focus is windows. The relationship established by Saul himself in giving his daughter to David as his wife is the very relationship that delivered David in his time of need. Even your enemy can be used by God to bless you or even set you up for deliverance.

The Apostle Paul was also delivered in his time of need by being let down in a basket, out of a window:

> *And through a window in a basket was I let down by the wall, and escaped his hands.*
>
> 2 Corinthians 11:33

While in the city of Damascus, the governor of the city sought to capture Paul. We see in both the Old and New Testament that God delivered His chosen men from those who would do them harm by lowering them from a window. There is deliverance in a window. God delivered the two spies, Rahab's family, David, and the Apostle Paul all with a window. God wants to set His people free from their past. He wants to set you free from the hurts of yesterday and from the mistakes that you keep playing over and over in your mind. God wants you to escape through the window and leave the past in the past once and for all. Now is the time for you to be set free from anything hindering you from fulfilling the call God Himself, has placed on your life. Right now, I want you to open the doors of your heart and raise your head to the windows of Heaven and receive the gifts the Lord has laid up for you. Take a moment and ask Him what He wants to set you free from right now.

God not only wants to deliver you, but He wants to deliver nations as well. Read this passage about the death of Jezebel:

> ³⁰*And when Jehu was come to Jezreel, Jezebel heard of it; and she painted her face, and tired her head, and looked out at a*

window. ³¹And as Jehu entered in at the gate, she said, Had Zimri peace, who slew his master? ³²And he lifted up his face to the window, and said, Who is on my side? who? And there looked out to him two or three eunuchs. ³³And he said, Throw her down. So they threw her down: and some of her blood was sprinkled on the wall, and on the horses: and he trode her under foot. ³⁴And when he was come in, he did eat and drink, and said, Go, see now this cursed woman, and bury her: for she is a king's daughter. ³⁵And they went to bury her: but they found no more of her than the skull, and the feet, and the palms of her hands. ³⁶Wherefore they came again, and told him. And he said, This is the word of the Lord, which he spake by his servant Elijah the Tishbite, saying, In the portion of Jezreel shall dogs eat the flesh of Jezebel: ³⁷And the carcase of Jezebel shall be as dung upon the face of the field in the portion of Jezreel; so that they shall not say, This is Jezebel.

2 Kings 9:30–37

God caused a just and upright man to arise and be bold. Jehu turned the situation around; he gave a decree and asked, "Who is with me?" Two or three of Jezebel's servants chose righteousness. These servants were in her bed chamber; she would have trusted them for them to be this close to her. One man stood up with the glory of God on his side and caused the queen's most trusted servants to throw her out a window. One man's influence caused a nation to be set free from Jezebel's tyranny.

5775, *Ayin Hey,* The Year of the Open Window is a time where the provision of 5773 and the relationships of 5774 merged, and God opened the windows of Heaven. God provided provision and He supplied it to doors, you and me. He then involved Heaven by blessing those relationships and providing divine revelation to those who have made room for Him in their heart. The picture of the *Hey* is a *Dalet,* a doorway with a hand reaching toward it. The hand reaching toward the doorway is God reaching out to you, empowering you, calling you to a higher level. Now is the time. Accept the call He has placed on your life. The time we are in is a season where He is pouring out His Spirit on all flesh. He is sharing His mysteries with His people unlike any other time in history. Let God get involved in your everyday routine. Let Him open your eyes to His mysteries.

Each year in this decade works together. In 5773, the camels began to be released to God's faithful people. In 5774, camels continued to come. God began to bring people into your life to establish covenant relationships. In 5775, camels were still coming, and the relationships established the previous year God began to get involved with. Promotions were and still are happening all across the body of Christ. They will continue throughout this entire decade. If it has not happened for you yet, just keep holding on to God and be patient. Promotion is coming.

During the year 5775, the ministry's nest egg began to run out. Tamara let us know that the money had dried up, and she was not going to go back to sleepless nights. She let us know it was time to pray and pray with a purpose. In October of 2014, another camel showed up by another anonymous giver. This time the gift was for $80,711.24. This gift was without stipulations, meaning we could use it anywhere we needed. Isn't God good? He knew the money had ran out and moved on someone's heart to send a gift when it was needed.

This same year God made a way for us to upgrade our master control. I had wanted to upgrade our master control since 2009. The average cost to do so was close to $1,000,000. Each year I would go to the National Association of Broadcasters (NAB), the largest broadcasting show in the world held in Las Vegas, Nevada, hoping and praying God would show me a way to upgrade our master control without costing a fortune. Each year I would find a better and less expensive way to do it. I had finally found a way to do it for $150,000. During our Spring Praise-A-Thon, we raised $30,000 toward our new master control, and I began to purchase parts. During our Fall Praise-A-Thon, we had another partner step up and offer our largest matching challenge ever. This partner offered a $60,000 matching pledge so we could upgrade the master control. Our partners stepped up. They showed their support to Watchmen Broadcasting by meeting the need. We were able to raise the $60,000 before the end of the Praise-A-Thon. Thank you, partners.

Soon the $80,711.24 had run out. It was March 18, 2015 Dorothy and Tamara were live on air filming *Club 36*, our flagship program. I saw the mailman had come in the station, and I checked to see what had come in. I saw an envelope I recognized. The anonymous givers who have given the large gifts to the ministry used a foundation to give us their gifts. I saw the envelope was from the foundation, and I paced back and forth debating on whether or not to open it. Dorothy and Tamara had just started a segment, and it felt like an eternity waiting for them to go to a song. I continued to pace back and forth. I couldn't take it any more; I had to know what was in the envelope. I opened it and found a check for $101,067.36. I about leaped out of my skin. I wanted to share it with Dorothy and Tamara, but they were still in their segment. I had to share it with someone. I went to the staff one at a time just handing them the check with no explanation just to see their faces. The entire staff knew before Dorothy and Tamara.

During this period of time, I began to serve on the TV Committee at NRB. I began to share what was happening at the ministry. I shared how we were able to build our new master control with three channels of play out for $150,000. Jaws began to drop. They asked how we did it and if I would be interested in sharing at NAB. Of course, I said yes. The relationships God had set up the year before by Dorothy endorsing me at NRB paid off. Because of the relationship established by Dorothy's influence, I was promoted again to speak at the largest broadcast show in the world. Let's go even further back in time. The provision that was provided in 5773 and continued for the next three years allowed the finances to be there so the ministry could upgrade the master control. Each year works together, and you will see over and over again where each year will affect the next.

Look back on the year 5775, September 25, 2014 – September 13, 2015 and see if God delivered you from something. Has He promoted you in some area of your life? Has He shared something with you that blew you away? The relationships He has provided you with, have they made you stronger? Have you become bolder in your faith? What are you doing today that a few years ago you thought would have been impossible for you to do?

Chapter 5

5775, A SHEMITAH YEAR
SEPTEMBER 25, 2014 – SEPTEMBER 13, 2015

5775, The year of the Open Window was a Shemitah year. We learn about the Shemitah in Leviticus:

> [1]*And the Lord spake unto Moses in mount Sinai, saying,*
> [2]*"Speak unto the children of Israel, and say unto them,*
> *'When ye come into the land which I give you, then shall the*
> *land keep a sabbath unto the Lord.* [3]*Six years thou shalt sow*
> *thy field, and six years thou shalt prune thy vineyard, and*
> *gather in the fruit thereof;* [4]*But in the seventh year shall be*
> *a sabbath of rest unto the land, a sabbath for the Lord: thou*
> *shalt neither sow thy field, nor prune thy vineyard.* [5]*That*
> *which groweth of its own accord of thy harvest thou shalt not*
> *reap, neither gather the grapes of thy vine undressed: for it*
> *is a year of rest unto the land.* [6]*And the sabbath of the land*
> *shall be meat for you; for thee, and for thy servant, and for*
> *thy maid, and for thy hired servant, and for thy stranger that*
> *sojourneth with thee,* [7]*And for thy cattle, and for the beast*
> *that are in thy land, shall all the increase thereof be meat.'"*
>
> Leviticus 25:1–7

The word Shemitah means to *release*.

RELEASE:

1. The Shemitah is to wipe away all debts. You are to release everyone who owes you anything from their debts.

2. You are to release your right to the land. You are not allowed to farm or cultivate the land for one year. You cannot reap a harvest or sell any of the produce that grows on the land during a Shemitah year. Everything grown during the Shemitah belongs to the community. You are to leave your gates open so the poor, widows, your servants, and workers can take freely anything that is grown for personal consumption.

3. As an individual and a nation during a Shemitah, you are to redirect your focus to grow closer to God. During this year, you are to totally trust God. The Jews would pack synagogues and study halls to study the Torah. During the Shemitah, you are to pursue your spiritual purpose. The main purpose of the Shemitah is for us to change our focus from faith in ourselves and our abilities to faith in God.

What a major shock to our Western culture and the American dream! We are taught to work continually in order to get ahead. That is not what God has intended for us at all. God wants us to trust and rest in Him for an entire year. For six years God let you do things your way and for one year He wants you to do it His way. As you focus on God during the Shemitah, He will give revelation into your kingdom purpose and He will also show you how to do what you have been doing for years more efficiently.

> *And this is the manner of the release: Every creditor that lendeth ought unto his neighbor shall release it; he shall not exact it of his neighbor, or of his brother; because it is called the Lord's release.*
>
> Deuteronomy 15:2

> [7]*"If there is among you a poor man of your brethren, within any of the gates in your land which the Lord your God is giving you, you shall not harden your heart nor shut your hand from your poor brother,* [8]*but you shall open your hand wide to him and willingly lend him sufficient for his need, whatever he needs.* [9]*Beware lest there be a wicked thought in your heart, saying, 'The seventh year, the year of release, is at hand,' and your eye be evil against your poor brother and you give him nothing, and he cry out to the Lord against you, and it become sin among you.* [10]*You shall surely give to him,*

*and your heart should not be grieved when you give to him,
because for this thing the Lord your God will bless you in all
your works and in all to which you put your hand. "For the
poor will never cease from the land; therefore I command
you, saying, 'You shall open your hand wide to your brother,
to your poor and your needy, in your land.'"*

Deuteronomy 15:7–11

The last day of the last month of the year all debts are to be released. The last month of the Hebrew calendar is the month of Elul, and the last day is the 29th. According to our calendar, the last day of the year 5775 was September 13, 2015. On this day, any debt not yet paid has to be released unto the Lord, and you can no longer lay claim to anything your fellow man owed you. If you harden your heart toward the poor, God will take His hand off of you due to sin.

God is getting us ready for a great revival. However, we have to let go of things in the past. We have to let the hurts and offenses of yesterday go. We can no longer hold grudges. People who hurt us have to be forgiven now. God does not only want us to forgive each other's financial debt, but all debts we feel someone owes us. We can no longer hold anything against anyone. Jesus came that we may be forgiven and redeemed. If we stand and do not forgive our brothers and sisters no matter the pain they have caused, then He will not stand and forgive us.

> ¹⁴*"For if ye forgive men their trespasses, your heavenly Father will also forgive you: ¹⁵But if ye forgive not men their trespasses, neither will your Father forgive your trespasses."*
>
> Mathew 6:14–15

5775, The Year of the Open Window was a Shemitah year. It was a time to grow closer to God. It was an ordained time set aside by the King of Kings and the Lord of Lords to meet you in the cool of the day and share with you His plans for your future. The great thing about God is even if we miss something, He still gives us an opportunity to get things right. You may not have forgiven everyone you were supposed to last year. You may still be holding on to hurts from your past. God wants to set you free from those right now. As you have been reading this book, you are truly beginning to see that God in everything. He is in every aspect of your life. Take a moment right now and ask Him who you are holding a grudge against. Ask Him to help you set that person free from your offense. Ask Him to set you free from holding on to the past that is preventing you from getting closer to Him.

The people who grabbed hold of the Shemitah and understood God's timing were able to accomplish extraordinary things last year. In the previous chapter, you read all of the miracles and accomplishments the ministry had. Many of you who are reading this are beginning to remember even the little things that at the time looked insignificant that happened last year. This past Hebrew year has been a season of the miraculous. God opened the windows of Heaven and poured out blessings you could not contain. God came and met you where you were and began to enlighten you and show you things you had never seen before. He did that through people who spent time in His word and brought forth a new on time word. He used your pastors, teachers, employers, family members, and of course Christian television. He also sent His Spirit to deliver you from your past. Have you noticed you are not struggling with things in this new season like you have previously? God is also delivering the nation. We see how in our current political race for the White House outsiders are leading the charge. God is raising up people like you and me who are saying enough is enough. Everyone running for the office of President all began during the Shemitah. This is not by chance. God is not finished with America, and only He can make it great again.

Look back at your life over the last Hebrew year 5775, The Year of the Open Window, a Shemitah year (September 25, 2014 – September 13, 2015). Were you enlightened in any way? Have you sensed a refreshing of God's spirit in your life? Did God show up in some way and set you free from things in your past? Were you promoted in any way? Was any of your debt wiped away? Were you able to pay things off? Did more money come your way in this season?

Chapter 6

Deeper Meaning of the Ayin

In Chapter 1, I gave a very brief explanation of the *Ayin* (70). I explained it as I understood it as it was relevant to the previous Hebrew years 5773 – 5775. As I began to study the upcoming Hebrew year 5776, I began to find more and more information on the *Ayin*. I had researched the *Ayin* briefly. I understood that for the current decade we are in, it meant that God had been watching and that He would continue to watch His people. He is looking for the faithful to promote. When Pastor Ray Popham came to the station in the year 5773, we were told God has been watching and now He is rewarding. We saw the rewards with the Camels that came to the station over the past three years:

1st Camel: $604,437.04 gift for a building for Watchmen Broadcasting.

2nd Camel: $25,000 gift to the ministry.

3rd Camel: $378,428.61 gift to the ministry.

4th Camel: $80,711.24 gift to the ministry.

5th Camel: $60,000.00 matching gift for a new master control.

6th Camel: $101,067.36 gift to the ministry.

We also saw promotion. Dorothy gave up a chance to be on the TV Committee of the NRB. She put my name in her place. Her sacrifice has been seen by God, and now her name is on the ballot to be voted on to the board of NRB this year. Dorothy isn't being offered a committee position that answers to a boar;, she is being voted onto a board that the very committee she wanted to be on has to answer to. Isn't God good? Because of relationships, I had the opportunity to speak at NAB. God is promoting his people in this season. We have seen it first hand here at the ministry.

As we move forward in the years to come, the *Ayin* will shift and take a new meaning. The first five years of this decade, God has been watching us. In the Scriptures, God's intimate knowledge of our lives is sometimes referred to as the "Eye of the Lord." Adonai's eyes are in every place, observing both the good and the evil (Prov. 15:3). The Lord's eyes focus throughout the whole earth to defend the righteous (2 Chr. 16:9) and to sustain and deliver those who are hoping in His lovingkindness and faithful mercy. This has been the focus of the *Ayin* for the past five years. As we move into the second half of the decade, its meaning will expand, and we will become involved by the choices we make from here on out.

THE MEANING OF AYIN[1]

The word *Ayin* means *eye, to see,* and by extension, to *understand and obey. Ayin* is also referred to as a light — not just a light like the sun, but a much brighter light — a divine light. It's a divine light that can only be seen through spiritual eyes. This light is believed to be hidden in the Torah and can only be seen by an inner eye. I believe the inner eye the Jewish people are talking about is the Holy Spirit. The Holy Spirit is the one who is given to us to comfort us and show us the mysteries of God."

---

1   Refer to Hebrew4Christians.com for further study.

The *Ayin* is pictured as having two eyes that connect to a common "optic nerve" that leads to the brain. There is an evil eye and there is a good eye. The two eyes represent our will, the ability to choose our actions. We can choose which eye to perceive things through. You can see the glass half empty or half full. The choice is yours. The *Ayin* is a representation of your heart or will.

The *Ayin* is a silent letter. The Jews believe the *Ayin* "sees" but does not "speak" and therefore represents the attitude of humility. On the other hand, *Ayin* can represent idolatry and slavery which are both born out of a heart of envy.

When perceiving through the evil eye of *Ayin*, a person becomes a slave to the purposes of sin. Rashi, a well known rabbi translates Numbers 15:39 as follows:

"This shall be fringes for you, and when you see it, you will remember all the commandments of the Lord to perform them, and you shall not wander after your hearts and after your eyes after which you are going astray."

Another way of saying this is that the heart and the eyes are the spies of the body: they lead a person to transgress; the eyes see, the heart covets, and the body transgresses. The Jews believe that a person is a miniature world. The eye reflects the world outside and reveals the world inside. A person's outlook reveals their inner character.

The eyes of *Ayin* are also called light and dark, good and evil, and positive and negative. At this point in time, we are being bombarded with stories of evil in the media. We hear about ISIS, terrorist plots, and shootings. We hear about #BlackLivesMatter and see attacks on our police. Negativity is at an all-time high, and it is a plan and a tactic of the enemy. The enemy wants you so focused on his distractions that you forget to focus on God. Our enemy understands the *Ayin*, and he knows how to get us to look through the evil or dark eye of the *Ayin*. He's a master at it. He has had thousands of years to perfect his technique. We may live a hundred years. I think he has an unfair advantage. I think God thinks he had an unfair advantage too and that's why He sent our Savior Jesus Christ to even the playing field.

Have you noticed that even our church leaders have been affected by the dark eye of the *Ayin*? How many doom and gloom sermons have we sat through over the past few years? How about all the controversy and teachings of the blood moons? Many have been teaching through fear and not faith. I am not coming against these men and women of God, and I never will. I am only making an observation in the teaching technique employed. It is extremely easy to see things through the dark eye of *Ayin*. I have to actively catch myself from looking through the dark eye. When we are constantly bombarded by media that has an ulterior motive, it is easy to be manipulated. We need to be very careful in the coming season when it comes to negative stories we hear in the media. We need to begin to see things through the light or good eye of *Ayin*.

When I first began studying the coming Hebrew year, I found websites all over the internet proclaiming the end of the world. They stated that before the end of September horrible things were going to happen. The list of negative events went on and on. I found myself getting sucked into the doom and gloom prophesies of the coming year. I started reading about the Illuminati and how they add 4,000 years to their dates as a code. Then, I read about the all-seeing eye above the pyramid on the back of the dollar bill. I also read about the roman numerals below the pyramid on the dollar bill equal 1776, representing the year the Declaration of Independence was signed. Illuminati teaching states that their messiah figure will come back in the year 5776. They believe that their messiah will place the capstone on his kingdom beginning this year of 5776. Their messiah is obviously the antichrist. The Hebrew year 5776 began September 14, 2015. Since that time, we have had a surge of terrorist attacks. That is how Satan works; he works through fear. The capstone that he's placing is a capstone of fear that will cause people to look for a savior. He will show up with his antichrist and fool many as he brings peace to a world in turmoil. The more I studied these theories, they became darker and darker. There was no hope in sight. One night while studying, Tamara came to me and said she heard the Lord say, "Don't look for treasure where there is none." God used my wife to get me to stop looking through the dark eye of *Ayin* and to focus on the good eye of *Ayin*.

Ayin, in essence, represents the free will and choice the Lord has given us. As we progress in this decade, we will be required to use our free will and make tough choices. We will have to be mindful of the evil that is all around us. Our focus, however, will have to be on the Lord. We are entering a time where Psalms 23 will be part of our everyday life:

> ¹*The Lord is my shepherd; I shall not want.*
>
> ²*He maketh me to lie down in green pastures: he leadeth me beside the still waters.*
>
> ³*He restoreth my soul: he leadeth me in the paths of righteousness for his name's sake.*
>
> ⁴*Yea, though I walk through the valley of the shadow of death, I will fear no evil: for thou art with me; thy rod and thy staff they comfort me.*
>
> ⁵*Thou preparest a table before me in the presence of mine enemies: thou anointest my head with oil; my cup runneth over.*
>
> ⁶*Surely goodness and mercy shall follow me all the days of my life: and I will dwell in the house of the Lord for ever.*
>
> Psalm 23

Verse four is what I really want you to focus on, "I will fear no evil." I want you to think about it this way: I will not focus on any evil. When we accept Jesus in our hearts and make Him the center of our lives, He becomes our shepherd. When He is our shepherd, He provides all our needs. He protects us and leads us in His righteousness — not for our sakes, but for His. He has marked us with His name; therefore, He has to protect us. It is not optional for Him; He must protect us because of His own name. He is with us always, and He comforts us when fear tries to torment us. He puts us on display in front of our enemies just to show them that He is God. If this is what God does, then why are we so focused on evil and not 100% focused on Him?

From this moment on, my prayer for you is that you will stop and think about what you allow in your eye and ear gates. I pray that as you begin to process all the information that is thrown at you, you will stop and choose the right eye of *Ayin* to see it through. I'm not saying don't watch the news or stop listening to prophets or church leaders who bring a word of warning about a disaster. Just take the information and look at it through the eye of light. Pray for the potential situations, and then let it go and let God be God. Stay focused on your calling and purpose, and don't let the enemy distract you with his negativity.

Chapter 7

5776, The Year of the Tent Peg or The Year Heaven Invades Earth

5776, The Year of the Tent Peg or The Year Heaven Invades Earth, began on September 14, 2015 and will conclude on October 2, 2016. We will look at the last two numbers of the year 7 and 6, or 70 and 6. The year is *Ayin* (70) Vav (6). *Ayin* literally means *eye* or *to see* and by extension, *to understand and obey*. The *Vav* is the sixth letter in the Hebrew alphabet and means *hook, tent peg, nail,* or *pin*. The number six is the number of completion. God created the the Heavens and the Earth in six days and rested on the seventh. Everything has six sides — top, bottom, right, left, front, and back. Six is also the number representing man; man was created on the sixth day. Man also works six days. As I studied the meaning of this year, I became fascinated with the *Vav* and its meaning.

The Hebrew language does not have the word *and*; instead, every time in Hebrew when they wanted to connect something together they would put a *Vav* on the beginning of the second word. The *Vav* is also used to change the tense of words; it connects the past, present, and future. The Torah has more than 4,000 laws established to make sure that it is an authentic, unadulterated copy of the word of God. A large number of these laws pertain to the *Vav*.

The *Vav* appears in scripture in the very first verse:

In the beginning God created the heaven and (**Vav**) *earth.*
Genesis 1:1 *(emphasis mine)*

When something shows up in scripture the first time, it signifies its meaning and its purpose throughout the rest of the scripture. Here the *Vav* connects the heaven and the earth; by joining the two, it implies a connection between spiritual and earthly matters. In Hebrew the *Vav* shows up as the 22nd letter in the Torah attached to the sixth word; it alludes to the creative connection between all of the letters (there are 22 letters in the

Hebrew alphabet). *Vav* is therefore the connection force of God, the divine "hook" that binds together heaven and earth.

The *Vav* is also connected to the Tabernacle:

> *⁹And thou shalt make the court of the tabernacle: for the south side southward there shall be hangings for the court of fine twined linen of an hundred cubits long for one side: ¹⁰And the twenty pillars thereof and their twenty sockets shall be of brass;* **the hooks of the pillars and their fillets shall be of silver.**
>
> Exodus 27:9–10 (emphasis mine)

Here the word *Vav* is used to represent the hooks of silver which fasten to posts (also called *amudim)* that held the curtain (also called *yeriah)* to the Tabernacle. The Tabernacle was the place of God's habitation while the Israelites traveled in the wilderness. The Torah is the place of habitation today of God's word. Therefore, the scribes developed the idea that the Torah scroll was to be constructed in the manner of the Tabernacle. They call each parchment sheet of a scroll a *yeriah,* named for the curtain of the Tabernacle and each column of text an *amud,* named for the posts of the Tabernacle's court. Now, since each curtain of the Tabernacle was fastened to its post by means of a silver hook (*Vav*), the scribes made each column of text to begin with a letter *Vav*, thereby hooking the text to the parchment.

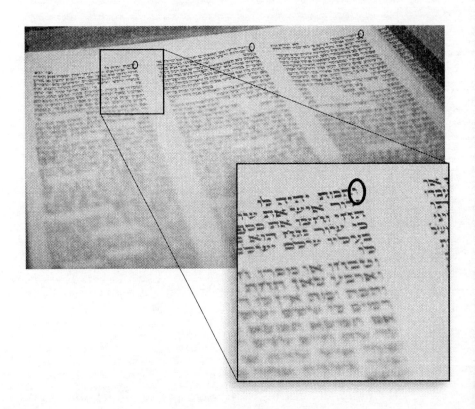

Some interesting facts about the *Vav* and its placement in the Torah are listed below:

> *Whatever crawls on its **belly**, whatever goes on all fours, or whatever has many feet among all creeping things that creep on the earth—these you shall not eat, for they are an abomination.*
>
> Leviticus 11:42 (emphasis mine)

In the center of the Torah is an oversized *Vav*, marking the center of the entire Torah. The word in which the *Vav* appears in is the word belly.

In Numbers we find the *Vav* is broken.

> *Wherefore say, "Behold I give unto him my covenant of **peace**..."*
>
> Numbers 25:12 (emphasis mine)

Here the *Vav* shows up broken. The laws for writing the Torah are extremely strict and require that all Hebrew letters be well formed. Letters cannot touch each other. Letter also cannot be malformed, broken, or illegible. It is strange that in the word *shalom* (peace) in the scripture above is broken. The Scribes choose to break the rules and place a broken *Vav*. Why is this *Vav* broken? The story this scripture comes from is when the Israelites were in Shittim, and they became seduced by the women of Moab and their gods. The Israelite men began to marry and join themselves to Baal of Peor. God called for the destruction of all that turned their back on Him. Now Zimri, an Israelite brought a Midianite woman who he was fornicating with in front of Moses and the rest of congregation in front of the Tabernacle of God. Phinehas, the grandson of Aaron, saw this and took a spear and thrust it through Zimri and the Midianite woman inside the tent of meeting. Because of Phinehas's zeal, the Lord's wrath was removed from the people. God then tells Moses: Behold I give unto him (Zimri) my covenant of peace. From a Messianic point of view, we can see Phinehas as a foreshadowing of Jesus. We can also think of the broken *Vav* as a picture of the brokenness of our Messiah for our ultimate deliverance. *Vav* is the number of man, and the broken *Vav* represents a man that is broken. The man has been broken for the sake of a covenant of peace that brought atonement to Israel.

Another place we find something interesting about the *Vav* is in Genesis:

> *These are the **generations** of the heavens and of the earth when they were created, in the day that the Lord God made the earth and the heavens.*
>
> Genesis 2:4 ***(emphasis mine)***

The *Vav* shows up in the word generations. The reference here in the generations is before the sin of man enters the world. Every other time the word generations (toldot) shows up referring to the genealogy of God's people the *Vav* is missing until Ruth 4:18:

> *Now these are the **generations** of Perez: Perrez begot Hezron..."*
>
> Ruth 4:18 ***(emphasis mine)***

The *Vav* reappears in the word generations here when the line of Perez is mentioned. This is very interesting. Why does the *Vav* show up before sin then show up again only in this one instance in scripture when Perez's family line is mentioned? The key is in the meaning of the name Perez. Perez means breach, or break through. God here is telling us that He is going to use Perez's line and break through mankind making way for our Messiah, Jesus Christ. Before sin entered the picture, the word for generation was spelled with the *Vav*. After sin entered, the *Vav* was removed. The *Vav* reappeared when God had chosen the man's lineage His son would derive from. Throughout the rest of scripture, the *Vav* is missing when the word generations appears.

THE MEANING OF THE VAV

The *Vav* has many meanings in the scripture. For this year the most well known and quoted instance occurs in Isaiah:

> *²Enlarge the place of your tent,*
> *And let them stretch out the curtains of your dwellings;*
> *Do not spare;*
> *Lengthen your cords,*
> *And strengthen your stakes.*
> *3For you shall expand to the right and to the left,*
> *And your descendants will inherit the nations,*
> *And make the desolate cities inhabited.*
>
> Isaiah 54:2–3

Now is the time to take the words the Lord has spoken over

you and do something about it. Make a plan and stretch beyond your limited abilities. Do not spare or hold anything back and strengthen your stakes or foundation. You are to expand in all directions. Look for areas that look dead and barren; now look at them through the positive eye of Ayin. New possibilities are being made known to you now that you overlooked before. They were hidden to you so they had time for you to mature in the things of the Lord. Now is your time to occupy what you thought was dead and gone.

Jabez prayed a prayer that many books have been written about:

> *⁹Now Jabez was more honorable than his brothers, and his mother called his name Jabez, saying, "Because I bore him in pain." ¹⁰And Jabez called on the God of Israel saying,* **"Oh, that You would bless me indeed, and enlarge my territory, that Your hand would be with me, and that You would keep me from evil, that I may not cause pain!"** *So God granted him what he requested.*
>
> 1 Chronicles 4:9–10 **(emphasis mine)**

What a simple prayer. God bless me, enlarge my territory,

put your favor on my life, keep evil away from me, and don't let me cause anyone pain. Jabez knew what his name meant. His whole life he was told he caused pain. What a horrible confession to make over a child. Jabez knew something had to change so he could enlarge his territory. He needed God to bless him, he needed God's favor, he needed the evil things spoken over his life removed from him, and he needed God to remove his old mindset. Jabez had a lifetime of thinking of himself as a person who brings others pain. This year God wants to do for you what He did for Jabez. He wants to remove your past and your negative mindsets about yourself.

The *Vav* shows up as a tent peg that delivered the Israelites in Judges:

> *¹⁷"However, Sisera had fled away on foot to the tent of Jael, the wife of Heber the Kenite; for there was peace between Jabin king of Hazor and the house of Heber the Kenite. ¹⁸And Jael went out to meet Sisera, and said to him, "Turn aside, my lord, turn aside to me; do not fear." And when he had turned aside with her into the tent, she covered him with a blanket. ¹⁹Then he said to her, "Please give me a little water to drink, for I am thirsty." So she opened a jug of milk, gave him a drink, and covered him. ²⁰And he said to her,*

> *"Stand at the door of the tent, and if any man comes and inquires of you, and says, 'Is there any man here?' you shall say, 'No.'"* ²¹ *Then Jael, Heber's wife,* **took a tent peg and took a hammer in her hand, and went softly to him and drove the peg into his temple, and it went down into the ground;** *for he was fast asleep and weary. So he died.* ²² *And then, as Barak pursued Sisera, Jael came out to meet him, and said to him, "Come, I will show you the man whom you seek." And when he went into her tent, there lay Sisera, dead with the peg in his temple.*
>
> Judges 4:17–22 ***(emphasis mine)***

In the previous verses, we learn that Barak was told to go and attack Sisera. He refused to do it unless the prophetess Deborah went with him. God honored Barak in the battle but took away the glory he should have received by being the one to kill Sisera. God used Deborah to tell Barak that a woman would get the glory for killing Sisera because he did not go when God told him to. Jael was a descendant of Moses' father-in-law. She was not an Israelite; she in essence could be considered as a gentile. Because Barak would not do as he was instructed, not only did God give the glory to a woman, but He gave it to an outsider.

God used something as simple as a tent peg to deliver His

people. God wants to deliver you from your past hurts, failures, mistakes, addictions, and misfortunes. The word of the Lord for this season is, **"Take your past and drive a stake through it."** Your past does not dictate your future! God is in control of your future. God is giving you power to redeem your past! He is giving you strategies to fulfill His promise of your future.

> [11]*"**For I know the thoughts that I think toward you, says the Lord, thoughts of peace and not of evil, to give you a future and a hope.** [12]Then you will call upon Me and go and pray to Me, and I will listen to you. [13]And you will seek Me and find Me, when you search for Me with all your heart. [14]I will be found by you, says the Lord, and I will bring you back from your captivity; I will gather you from all the nations and from all the places where I have driven you, says the Lord, and I will bring you to the place from which I cause you to be carried away captive."*
>
> Jeremiah 29:11–14 *(emphasis mine)*

God already had a plan to save you before you got in trouble. The second you turn your heart towards Him, He is there to deliver you. You will find Him in this new season as soon as you look for Him. He wants to make Himself known to you.

Let us now take what we have learned about the *Ayin* (70) and the *Vav* (6) and apply it to the Year of the Tent Peg, or the Year Heaven Invades Earth. This year God wants to deal with your mindset. He wants you to focus all of your thoughts away from the evil or negative eye of *Ayin* to the eye of light or the positive eye of *Ayin*. The evil eye of *Ayin* is where our enemy manipulates us with fear, timidity, unbelief, weakness, hopelessness, passively, and poverty. The opposite of faith is fear. Fear is actually a perverted version of faith. Fear is you looking through the evil eye of *Ayin* and focusing on the worst case scenario. Fear is a total lack of trust in our Heavenly Father. Satan fills some people with fear and timidity. He makes you think you could never do that. God could never use you in a special way. You're just a timid person. It's time to break that mindset. It's time to put a tent peg in those old mindsets! Paul instructs us:

> *For God hath not given us the spirit of fear; but of power, and of love, and of a sound mind.*
>
> 2 Timothy 1:7

Another tool of the enemy is unbelief and feeling we are

weak. As long as you look at situations through the dark eye of Ayin, you will never believe that God has a plan and a purpose for you. Unbelief is thinking good things can't happen to me. Well I am here to tell you that God wants to use you as a power house in His kingdom. It's time to do away with unbelief and the feeling of weakness. **Take your tent peg and drive it through your weakness and unbelief!**

> *I have strength for all things in Christ Who empowers me [I am ready for anything and equal to anything through Him Who infuses inner strength into me; I am self-sufficient in Christ's sufficiency].*
>
> Philippians 4:13 AMP

God has set you up to do greater things than Jesus did. All you have to do is believe. You are sufficient. God dwells on the inside of you. Inside of you is a roaring lion waiting to get out.

Sometimes we may feel foolish saying things over and over and not seeing the manifestation of what we believe for. Now is the time to call those things that are not as though they are again. Even though you may feel foolish, you are wiser than any man on the planet because you are tapping into the power of the One who created the universe.

[This is] because the foolish thing [that has its source in] God is wiser than men, and the weak thing [that springs] from God is stronger than men.

1 Corinthians 1:25 AMP

Even the great Apostle Paul had times when he felt insufficient. What you think is weakness, God sees as an opportunity to show off how mighty He really is. Inside your weakness is your greatest strength. It is at your weakest that you truly rely on God the most.

8 Three times I called upon the Lord and besought [Him] about this and begged that it might depart from me; 9 But He said to me, My grace (My favor and loving-kindness and mercy) is enough for you [sufficient against any danger and enables you to bear the trouble manfully]; for My strength and power are made perfect (fulfilled and completed) and show themselves most effective in [your] weakness. Therefore, I will all the more gladly glory in my weaknesses and infirmities, that the strength and power of Christ (the Messiah) may rest (yes, may pitch a tent over and dwell) upon me! 10 So for the sake of Christ, I am well pleased and take pleasure in infirmities, insults, hardships, persecutions, perplexities and distresses; for when I am weak [in human strength], then am I [truly] strong (able, powerful in divine strength).

2 Corinthians 12:8–10 AMP

Our enemy wants you to feel hopeless. He wants to beat you down. He wants you focusing on the evil eye of *Ayin*. He wants you to hear the news that disaster is coming. He wants you to prophesy doom and gloom over your life. *I will never break through. My situation will never change. God has passed me by.* These are thoughts he has planted in you to hold you in bondage and prevent you from fulfilling your destiny. Tell the enemy, "Enough is enough!" Take your tent peg, drive it through his temple, and kill those mindsets once and for all.

Now that you have made the choice to renew your mindsets, here are some verses for you to stand on.

> *Many are the afflictions of the righteous: but the Lord delivereth him out of them all.*
>
> Psalms 34:19

> *They do not fear bad news; they confidently trust the lord to care for them.*
>
> Psalms 112:7 NLT

> *¹God is our refuge and strength, a very present help in trouble. ²Therefore will not we fear, though the earth be removed, and though the mountains be carried into the midst of the sea;*
>
> Psalms 46:1–2

¹Bless the Lord, O my soul: and all that is within me, bless his holy name.

²Bless the Lord, O my soul, and forget not all his benefits:

³Who forgiveth all thine iniquities; who healeth all thy diseases;

⁴Who redeemeth thy life from destruction; who crowneth thee with lovingkindness and tender mercies;

⁵Who satisfieth thy mouth with good things; so that thy youth is renewed like the eagle's.

Psalms 103:1–5

This year, as your mind is renewed, your faith will activate in a way it never has before. You will believe the Word of the Lord more than you ever have before. You will begin to understand things that you have always had questions about. We are entering a supernatural season, and angels are going with us. We are entering a season of great warfare, but we will be protected. The eyes of God search the earth for those He can show His mighty strength through, those who truly are His. It's a season where the relationship He has established will flourish, and greater promotion will come. God is ready to show His power through you this year. This year Heaven will invade Earth.

God is dealing with your past this year so it will not hinder your future. You are to enlarge your tent and expand in every direction. God is redeeming past opportunities for you now. You will start with a clean slate this year if you redirect your focus from the negativity of the evil Ayin to the good eye of Ayin. Heaven is invading the Earth; your season is about to change. When God gets involved and heaven comes down, our enemy will be dealt with. He will establish His people. We will TRANSITION, REPOSITION, and PLUNDER THE ENEMY. God is connecting us to heaven, and all the things heaven holds, we can call in this season. The windows of heaven are open to us now. Start calling in the promises of the Lord.

The *Vav* this year will allow us to connect to heaven, but it will also connect the past, present, and future. I have already explained to you that your past will be wiped away. Now I want to show you that you can pull the future into the present. In the Old Testament, David brought the Ark of the Covenant back to the Israelites. He constructed a new tent for the Ark and established praise and worship around the clock. God honored

David and his zeal for the things of God, and the people where allowed to come into the glory of the Lord for a 40-year period. This is a new covenant promise. How were the Israelites able to enter the glory of the Lord? God so loved David that He reached forward in time and pulled a portion of the new covenant into the past to honor David for his love of the Lord. The good news is that in this season you and I can do the same thing. We can pull things from the next age into the past. Signs and wonders from the millennial reign are waiting for you and me to bring them into this present age. Heaven is ready to invade the Earth.

The year is *Ayin* (70) *Vav* (6) and heaven is invading earth. You have the option of redeeming your past or repeating it for another season. Everything in your past that you think has held you back will lose its hold on you this year. You are going to reach into the future and pull in signs and wonders, showing God immense power. You will overcome the enemy this year. God will establish you as His people and transition and reposition you to where you should have already been. He will allow you to plunder the enemy for His sake. As you pray this year, you will have more authority, and you, the *Vav*, (the number six, the number representing man) will be used to connect heaven to earth. You are the connecting pin that God is going to use to usher the invasion of heaven on earth. This year you will use the *Vav*, the tent peg, and NAIL DOWN and SECURE YOUR FUTURE! This is a year to EXTEND YOUR BOARDERS! A year to EXPAND YOUR VISION! A year to STAKE A CLAIM FOR YOUR FUTURE! This is the year you plant your tent stake in the ground and see the gates of your future open. It's time to LET GOD ESTABLISH YOUR FUTURE!

What has already happened in your life since September 14, 2015? You know everything you are reading is true. Your spirit man is ready to leap out of you; he is so excited. You have been sensing something is happening in the supernatural, but you didn't know what it was. How has God redeemed you from your past? What mindsets have you set aside? What are you going to put a stake in and leave in the past? What is God telling you to pull from the future to the here and now?

Chapter 8

Year of Jubilee

5776, the Year of the Tent Peg is also a Jubilee Year. Earlier we learned about the Shemitah. The Shemitah happens every seven year. The Jubilee year happens at the end of seven Shemitahs.

*⁸'And **you shall count seven sabbaths of years for yourself**, seven times seven years; and the time of the seven sabbaths of years shall be to you forty-nine years. ⁹Then you shall cause the trumpet of the Jubilee to sound on the tenth day of the seventh month; on the Day of Atonement you shall make the trumpet to sound throughout all your land. ¹⁰And **you shall consecrate the fiftieth year, and proclaim liberty throughout all the land to all its inhabitants. It shall be a Jubilee for you; and each of you shall return to his possession, and each of you shall return to his family**. ¹¹That fiftieth year shall be a Jubilee to you; in it **you shall neither sow nor reap what grows of its own accord**, nor gather the grapes of your untended vine. ¹²For it is the Jubilee; it shall be holy to you; you shall eat its produce from the field. ¹³'In this Year of Jubilee, each of you shall return to his possession**. ¹⁴And if you sell anything to your* *neighbor or buy from your neighbor's hand, you shall not oppress one another. ¹⁵According to the number of years after the Jubilee you shall buy from your neighbor, and according to the number of years of crops he shall sell to you. ¹⁶According to the multitude of years you shall increase its price, and according to the fewer number of years you shall diminish its price; for he sells to you according to thenumber of the years of the crops. ¹⁷Therefore you shall not oppress one another, but you shall fear your God; for I am the Lord your God."*

Leviticus 25:8–17 NKJV *(emphasis mine)*

Many call the Jubilee a super Shemitah. The same rules apply, no farming, the land is to rest. You are to trust the Lord for an entire year and grow closer to Him. You are to forgive any and all debts. What is different during the Jubilee is that if you sold your families' land or yourself into slavery during the Jubilee, you are to be restored. Everything you or your family lost was to be restored every 50 years. God knew we would give in to our flesh. He knew we would over extend ourselves and end up in bondage if we were left to our own devices. He provided a way where every generation could be restored and start over free from any and all bondage.

September 14, 2015 through October 2, 2016 is a Jubilee year. Let's take a look at the last time land was restored to the nation of Israel. That was 1967, the Six Day War in which Jerusalem was restored to Israel. Here we are seven Shemitahs later; we have entered another Jubilee year.

In the previous chapter, we learned about the *Ayin* (70) and the *Vav* (6) and how they will affect this year. Now that we know that this year is a Jubilee year, the redemption from the past begins to make a lot more sense as we begin to understand God's calendar. In a Jubilee year, all past outstanding debts were absolved. This year God wants to redeem your past. Do you see the correlation? During a Jubilee year, you are to trust God for everything and grow closer to Him. This year God wants to reveal to you His great mysteries. He wants to show you new things and a better way of doing things. Now is the time for you to get in agreement with God and put your tent stake in the ground to secure the future He has for you.

During a Jubilee year, the Israelites would partake of trees they planted years earlier and never harvested. How many seeds have you planted over the years? How many of them have not yet produced fruit? During a Jubilee, they would eat of plants that produced on their own. They would not harvest anything, but they would take what they needed as they needed it. Their fields would be open for anyone who was hungry to come and partake of what grew unattended. You have planted seeds over the years that the Lord has prompted you to, but you have not yet seen the return. I am telling you now by the Spirit of the Lord that those seeds you have sown sacrificially were for a purpose. They will begin to manifest and bring in their intended harvest now in this new season you are about to enter. Some plants take several years before they sprout and several more before producing anything. The Chinese Bamboo tree takes five years before it breaks through the ground. However, once it breaks through the ground in a period of five weeks the tree can reach a height of ninety feet. The seeds you have sown are about to breakthrough and set you up for your future.

In this Jubilee year, you need to take heed, listen, and make preparations. This is a year for you to truly understand your purpose. In this season, you will get clarity and make advancements for the kingdom. The Jubilee signals the beginning of a new Shemitah cycle. You will continue to get more and more clarity over the next seven years as we move into a new Shemitah cycle. As God blesses you in this new season, your focus needs to be set on getting out of debt. The choices you make this year need to be carefully thought out and made with purpose. Take heed of what is around you. Pay attention to all of your options. Listen to the still, small voice inside you. Then, act on it, making preparation for your future.

Your lost loved ones are coming home during this year of Jubilee. When the Israelites would sell themselves into slavery, their family would be separated. In this season, God is restoring the family. He is bringing your loved ones back home. Get ready for the prodigal sons and daughters; they are coming home this year. God is restoring every aspect of your life that has been surrendered to the enemy. You are no longer a slave to sin. You are no longer going to be held in bondage. The Great Deliverer is here to set you free. Everything ever stolen from you or your family line over a thousand generations will be returned to you beginning now this year, the year of Jubilee.

As the Lord begins to restore what has been stolen from you, you may become overwhelmed. As God begins to open doors for you, as He returns stolen properties, you may be asking, how am I going to accomplish or keep up with all of these blessings and new responsibilities. The answer is simple; you will begin to occupy a small section at a time. Just take one step at a time. No matter how small the step is, know that wherever your foot touches now belongs to the kingdom of heaven. Start looking at things in phases. You do not eat an elephant all at once. You cut off a section at a time. The same is true in this new season, take things in phases, and layout planned steps with purpose.

Has God already begun to bring loved ones back into your life this year? Are you having new opportunities offered to you? Are you starting to feel the need to plan things out? Have you begun to feel the urgent need to get out of debt? Have you noticed that blessings keep showing up out of nowhere? It is only the beginning!

Chapter 9

5777 THE YEAR OF THE PLOW OR THE SWORD

5777 the Year of the Plow or the Sword, begins October 3, 2016, and will conclude September 21, 2017. We will look at the last two numbers, the 7 and 7 or 70 and 7. The year is *Ayin* (70) *Zayin* (7). *Ayin* literally means *eye* or *to see* and by extension, *to understand and obey*. We also learned it means that as we move throughout the rest of this decade that we must choose which eye of the *Ayin* we will perceive through. Our future now depends on which eye we look through, the positive eye of *Ayin* or the negative eye of *Ayin*. Now that we know that our internal perspective is what will dictate our future, we now turn to the *Zayin* (7) to see what God has planned for the coming year. The *Zayin* is the seventh letter in the Hebrew alphabet and means *plow, food, weapon, kill, cut off,* and *death*. According to BibleStudy.org, "used 735 times (54 times in the book of Revelation alone), the number 7 is the foundation of God's word. If we include with this count how many times 'sevenfold' (6) and 'seventh' (119) is used, our total jumps to 860 references."[1]

In Chapter 6, we covered in great detail the meaning of the *Ayin* and how it will play out the rest of this decade. The most important thing you have to remember as you move forward is that your choices will have consequences, good or bad. How you see things will dictate your future. Are you easily manipulated by the media or by your friends to see things through their point of view, or are you filtering things through God's point of view? Think of a still photography camera. The lenses on these cameras can be changed to achieve different results. The standard lens that comes with the camera gives the photographer a wide angle allowing them to see everything in front of them. This is good to see the overall scene, but this also allows things that can distract the photographer from the desired result. Photographers carry many different lenses; one of the lenses they carry is a telephoto lens, which allows them to be very far away from something and

---

1   "Meaning of Numbers in the Bible The Number 7." Meaning of the Number 7 in the Bible. Barnabas Ministers / BibleStudy.org. Web. 25 Apr. 2016.

to take a photo as though they were right next to their subject. Think of the eyes of *Ayin* the same way. When you use the wide angle lens, you see everything, including all the distractions of the enemy. The wide angle is the evil eye of the *Ayin*; it prevents you from focusing on the things of God and hinders your relationship with Him. Pretend for one minute that there is a mountain in the distance you desire to go to. You can see it, but it is so far away. You also see everything in your way, keeping you from reaching your destination. With all of the distractions in your way you feel as though you will never reach your destination. Now take the telephoto lens and look at the mountain. The mountain now appears so close you can reach out and touch it. Everything that has been holding you back is no longer in view. This is how things appear when you look through the good eye of *Ayin*.

THE IMPORTANCE OF THE NUMBER SEVEN

The number seven is a very powerful and fundamental number to God. The seven represents a sword. What does a sword do? A sword cuts and divides. Just looking at how we understand time, we see how vital the number seven is. There are seven days in a week. Every seventh year is holy unto the Lord, hence the Shemitah. After seven Shemitahs, we have the year of Jubilee. All of the Jewish festivals occur within the first seven months of the year. We are awaiting the seventh millennium where we will rule with Christ Jesus during the Millennial Reign. In these examples we see how important the number seven is. We learned earlier that the number six represents completion. The number seven represents completed perfection. Why did God create the earth in six days and rest on the seventh? I believe that He worked the six days, and on the seventh He admired what He had created. God worked the six days, and completed creation. He gave the seventh day His blessing and approval, making it a completed, perfected creation.

The *Zayin* (7) is a very interesting letter in the Hebrew Alphabet. The *Zayin* looks like a *Vav* (6) with a crown on top of it. The *Vav* is a masculine letter; the Jews believe that it represents a direct light from God to man. The *Zayin* is a feminine letter; the Jews believe that it represents a light reflecting back. A famous Rabbi from the 1700s named Baal Shem Tov refers to the *Zayin* this way, "Just as a woman of valor is the crown of her husband, so *Zayin* the seventh letter is the crown of the *Vav*."[2]

> *An excellent wife is the crown of her husband,*
> *But she who causes shame is like rottenness in his bones.*
>
> Proverbs 12:4 NKJV

THE MEANING OF ZAYIN

The *Zayin* represents a sword and a plow. Both of these instruments cut, but they are used for different purposes. The Sword is used to fight, kill, and deliver. The plow is used to cut the ground to provide nourishment and sustenance. The *Zayin* brings life through death and nourishment through the sword. It breaks up ground for the purpose of bringing forth seed. *Zayin* cuts deep into the soul to cut out what is not of Him so that new life can sprout. While studying the *Zayin*, I came across a minster named Jim Stanley who had studied a great deal on the Hebrew alphabet. As I watched his sermons, I learned lot of very interesting things about the *Zayin*. The human heart is divided into four quadrants, but when it is

---

2   Parsons, John J. "The Letter Zayin." The Letter Zayin. Hebrew for Christians. Web. 25 Apr. 2016.

cut in half, it actually is shaped like the two stone tablets the Ten Commandments are on.

> *¹⁸Therefore you shall lay up these words of mine in your heart and in your soul, and bind them as a sign on your hand, and they shall be as frontlets between your eyes. ¹⁹You shall teach them to your children, speaking of them when you sit in your house, when you walk by the way, when you lie down, and when you rise up.*
>
> Deuteronomy 11:18–19

> *Bind them on your fingers;*
> *Write them on the tablet of your heart.*
>
> Proverbs 7:3

> *²⁰My son, keep your father's command,*
> *And do not forsake the law of your mother.*
> *²¹Bind them continually upon your heart;*
> *Tie them around your neck.*
> *²²When you roam, they will lead you;*
> *When you sleep, they will keep you;*
> *And when you awake, they will speak with you.*
> *²³For the commandment is a lamp,*
> *And the law a light;*
> *Reproofs of instruction are the way of life.*
>
> Proverbs 6:20–23

When you think about these scriptures and realize that your heart could actually resemble the very stones that the commandments were written on, these verses take on a whole new meaning. The more we look into Judaism, the deeper the meanings we can pull from the word of God. All throughout history, God has spoken to His people through pictures. That's why each letter has a picture and a number value attached to it to make things simple for us to understand. The word of God states that "my people perish for a lack of knowledge." There is way more to the word of God than what we take at face value just reading the stories and accounts.

All through out history, all around the world, we have been told stories about how people were oppressed by their leaders or rival nations. Farmers would rise up and take their farming equipment and plows, to make weapons to deliver themselves or their nation. So is it any wonder that the *Zayin* would represent both a sword and a plow. The sword of *Zayin* from a worldly perspective is believed to represent the survival of the fittest. The world is set up in a way that we are constantly battling to get ahead or to succeed in this world. The sword from a divine perspective becomes a royal scepter. By overcoming the struggles of the world and by His enlightenment through those struggles, God is in control and is moving the world forward. On an even deeper level it is said God is providing for everyone all of life.

In Matthew 10:34 Jesus tells us why He came to earth:

> *Do not think that I came to bring peace on earth. I did not come to bring peace but a sword.*
>
> Matthew 10:34

Jesus did not come to bring peace to the earth on His first trip here. He came to bring the sword. Why would He bring a sword? What sword did He bring? Jesus came to bring the Sword of the Spirit.

> *And take the helmet of salvation, and the sword of the Spirit, which is the word of God.*
>
> Ephesians 6:17

> *For the word of God is living and powerful, and sharper than any two-edged sword, piercing even to the division of soul and spirit, and of joints and marrow, and is a discerner of the thoughts and intents of the heart.*
>
> Hebrews 4:12

The word of God is the Sword of the Spirit. Jesus is the fulfillment of the word of God. Everything in the Old Testament is a foreshadowing of the coming of Jesus the Christ. The whole New Testament is based on His coming and a greater understanding of what He did on the cross. Jesus is the word of God and the word of God is the Sword of the Spirit.

Earlier I told you that when your heart is cut in two, it appears as the shape of two stone tablets. Let's look at a plow and how it separates the earth. When a plow is placed into the ground it separates the earth; the dirt is placed on both sides of the hole that was just created. Seed is then placed into the hole that was created by the plow. The plow breaks up the hard ground giving the seed a chance to grow in soft ground.

> *³Then He spoke many things to them in parables, saying: "Behold, a sower went out to sow. ⁴And as he sowed, some seed fell by the wayside; and the birds came and devoured them. ⁵Some fell on stony places, where they did not have much earth; and they immediately sprang up because they had no depth of earth. ⁶But when the sun was up they were scorched, and because they had no root they withered away. ⁷And some fell among thorns, and the thorns sprang up and choked them.*

> *⁸But others fell on good ground and yielded a crop: some a hundredfold, some sixty, some thirty. ⁹He who has ears to hear, let him hear!"*
>
> Matthew 13:3–9

Just as the sower plants his seed, the Lord has planted seed in us. However, many of us have not allowed Him to use His plow to prepare our hearts for the seeds He has for us. We have refused to heed His word. He wants to open our hearts. He will open our hearts one of two ways. He will either open them with the sword or with the plow. Sometimes a farmer has to clear the land and cut back growth that is undesired in order to prepare the ground for a harvest. God does the same; sometimes we have allowed so many thorns and weeds into our lives that God has to come and utterly cut them out of us before He can use His plow to soften our hearts so He can put seeds in us that will produce a great harvest.

Now that we know what the *Zayin* means, let's apply it to where we are in time. 5775 was a Shemitah year in which the land was to rest. 5776 is a Jubilee year which is also a Shemitah year where the land is to rest. For the past two years in the natural, the land has rested. During the Jubilee anything you or your family has lost since the last year of Jubilee is to be restored to you. That is great news that your inheritance is coming back to you! However, what state is your inheritance in? Did the person you sell your inheritance to take care of your property, or did they become overwhelmed and let it go? This year God is calling us to pull out our plow and get to work. There are areas in your life that you need to prepare for a harvest. As in the natural, the land has rested for two years, and it is ready to be worked; the same goes for you in your natural, and spiritual life. Now is the time to get to work. Let the dreams and visions the Lord has given you come into fruition.

5777 is the year God wants you to use your plow and to work the gifts, and talents He has given you for His purposes. If you put out the evil, dark, and negative eye of *Ayin* and focus instead on the plans God has for you this year, you will experience more growth than any other time in your life. Jesus came to give you life and give it abundantly. The enemy comes to kill, steal, and destroy. Even though you are working and nurturing the relationship you have with God to find the ultimate purpose He has placed in you, the enemy will continue to attack. He will look for opportunities to discourage you. Don't forget that this is also the year of the sword. Jesus came to bring the sword, the Sword of the Spirit; He has equipped you with all of the tools you need to be a conqueror and an overcomer. In the book of Nehemiah, we read about the story of the Israelites rebuilding the wall in the city of Judah. While building the wall, the Samaritans would come, and make life difficult for the Hebrews. They would bribe officials to slow down the building process. They would try to tear down the wall and threaten the lives of those who were rebuilding the wall. Why were they so opposed to the rebuilding of the wall? In the book of Ezra we learn that the treasures of the Trans-Euphrates was responsible to pay for whatever the Jews needed to rebuild the city of Jerusalem. They opposed it because they were responsible for the cost of rebuilding it. Nehemiah told the people of Judah to work with one hand and hold a weapon in the other. Even though the Lord has given you back what belongs to you, the enemy is not happy about it; he will try to stop you at all cost. Later the people complained about having to hold a weapon while they worked. Nehemiah then chose people to hold weapons and to watch over those who were working. We can't complete everything God has for us on our own. It is very difficult to work and to fight at the same time. There may be a time where you are the one working, and you have someone watching over you. At other times, you may be the one watching over someone who is working. What is important is that you can discern the times when you need to be the worker or the warrior. It is important that you realize which one you need to be at what time. You may be both the worker and the warrior. The enemy is not happy, and he will show up angry with his false acquisitions and lies. In this season, God is going to use your enemy to pay for everything He has for you to do. God has not only returned everything stolen from you, and your family, but He is making your enemy pay the bill for getting it ready to produce a great harvest. We serve a good God.

Have you noticed that you have favor on your life in this season unlike any other time in your life? Are your enemies fighting, but getting nowhere? Does it seem the harder they fight, the more they end up bringing blessings to you? What they mean for your destruction is causing you to be catapulted to new levels! God is turning your sword into a scepter and giving you great authority over your enemy.

Chapter 10

Closing Remarks

My prayer is that the information in this book has empowered you to fulfill the call God has placed on your life. I pray that you are encouraged and made stronger through the words on these pages. I believe God will supply all your needs according to His riches in Christ Jesus. I pray the camels of 5773 will continue to enter your life and make a way for your purpose. I am also standing in agreement with you that the doors of relationships that God has established and restored in 5774 will continue to grow into deeper, covenant relationships. I know that the windows of heaven in 5775 have been opened over you, and promotions have come your way. I also believe more promotions are coming your way. As we move through 5776, I pray your eyes will see and process things and events through the good or light eye of *Ayin*. I know you are being redeemed from your past.

I pray you use your tent stake and drive it into the past and let go of any mindsets that have prevented you from moving into the future designed for you by the Creator Himself. I know that provisions from seeds sown when it hurt to do so will manifest in this season. I also know that your prodigals are coming home. I pray your FAITH expands this year like never before. I pray your HOPE and TRUST in the Lord take the main stage in your life this year. I pray that you become BOLD and FEARLESS NOW in the name of Jesus.

I want to hear about what God has done in your life. Please send me your stories. I would love to hear about the goodness of God and the mighty things He has done for you. You can send your testimonies to info@wbpi.org.

ABOUT THE AUTHOR

Chris James received his degree in film and video with a minor in sound deign from the Savannah College of Art and Design in Savannah, Georgia. In 2002 Chris was employed at Watchmen Broadcasting, working in every department in the nonprofit television ministry include production, fund raising, IT, engineering, and management. While working at Watchmen Chris began to excel in technology and was asked to join the NRB TV Committee, and speak at NAB. In 2004 Chris married Tamara Luscombe, the Vice President of Watchmen Broadcasting. They have two children they are raising in the ministry. Chris hosts a prayer program at Watchmen Broadcasting called It's Time To Pray as well as co-host Watchmen's flagship program Club 36. After interviewing pastors, about Hebraic times, and seasons, Chris has become fascinated with the Hebraic way of seeing things in the Bible. Now he spends countless hours studying all he can about the Hebrew calendar, the numbers, alphabet, and feast times and seasons to better understand the times we are living in.

If you would like to have Chris James speak at your church or event you can contact him at:

Watchmen Broadcasting
PO Box 3618
Augusta, GA 30914

(803) 278-3618

chris@wbpi.org